The Wind and the Sun

Retold and dramatised from the
Aesop's fable as a reading play
for partners or small groups.

Ellie Hallett

Ways to read this story

This story is suitable for school and home. Some 'how to read' ideas are below.

- With a partner or small group, take it in turns to read the rows.

- Don't rush! This helps you to say each word clearly.

- Think of yourselves as actors by adding lots of facial and vocal expression. Small gaps of silence also create dramatic energy. These techniques will bring the story to life.

- If you meet a new word, try to break it down and then say it again. If you have any problems, ask your teacher or a reading buddy.

- Don't be scared of unusual words. They will become your new best friends.
  (New words strengthen your general knowledge and enable you to become vocabulary-rich in your day-to-day life.)

Have fun!

Unknown artist

One day the Wind and the Sun
argued as to who was the stronger.

'I am certainly mightier than you,
Sun. I can push out my cheeks,
puff myself up, and B-L-O-W!'

Straight away leaves fell off trees and scattered everywhere.

People's hats came off while their owners chased after them.

Boats at sea began rocking from side to side.

Birds stopped singing and looked for a place to shelter.

'There you are, Sun. How's that for strength and power?'

And Wind looked proudly at the clouds as they raced and scudded across the sky.

'You may think that all I do is quietly shine all day while you push and blow and shake.'

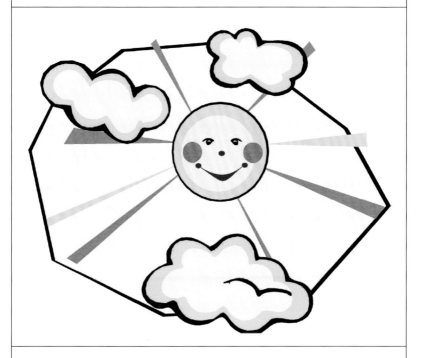

'My sunlight is also powerful. It helps small seeds grow into crops and forests.'

'I open the flower buds for the bees.'

'My heat and light make the world green and beautiful.'

Wind replied with disdain in his voice and contempt in his gusty words …

'If that's what you think, Sun, let's have a contest.'

'My strength will prove to us both who really is the toughest and strongest and mightiest around here!'

Sun spoke gently to Wind.

'What a good idea, Wind. A contest will be the fairest way to prove that I'm a great deal stronger than you might think!'

'Ha ha! Prepare yourself to lose, and lose badly, Sunshine.'

And Wind chuckled so fiercely that smoke from the nearby house chimneys blew sideways in a rush.

Sun looked down calmly onto the Earth while Wind hurried and blustered in all directions.

With a sudden gust of excitement, Wind saw a way to prove that he was by far the stronger.

'Do you see that man travelling along the road wearing a coat?'

'The first to force that man's coat off him will be the winner.'

'That traveller looks very experienced at being out in all weathers.

Blowing his coat off could be a difficult task!'

'No worries! I'll blow that coat off him before you can say southerly buster! So you agree that this will be a fair test of strength, Sun?'

'Yes, I agree. I will now disappear for a while until it is my turn to do what I do best. The stronger of us will be known as the winner!'

Wind rushed over to where the traveller was walking along the road to the next town.

The man whistled a merry tune as he walked along happily.

Wind began blowing and puffing and pushing him rather roughly.

The man stopped whistling.

He looked up at the sky to check this sudden change in the weather.

Wind decided to blow a little harder.

The traveller pulled his hat down more tightly.

He did up all the buttons of his coat to stop it flapping.

Wind knew he'd have to blow very fiercely to win this contest.

Great whirlwinds of spinning air swirled and pushed around the road.

The traveller held onto his coat more tightly than before.

He was puzzled at how this nasty cold wind seemed to come from nowhere.

Children rushed home from school as quickly as they could.

Meanwhile, Sun watched quietly from behind the gathering clouds

White-caps appeared on the waves at sea.

But Wind was not beaten yet. He decided to blow harder.

He tried near gale.

The children and mothers and dogs and cats ran indoors to escape the fury.

Wind then tried full gale.

The trees bent so much that they almost touched the ground.

Finally, Wind tried storm.

The captains on the ships at sea warned passengers not to go out onto the open decks.

The traveller held onto his coat ever more tightly.

Luckily, he was able to find shelter from the Wind in the safety of a strong, thick hedge beside the road.

He wrapped his collar around his face for protection.

And still Wind roared like a thousand demons.

Twigs and small branches snapped off trees.

A yacht in the harbour blew right over.

Birds and insects sheltered in barns and sheds.

And the traveller held onto his coat as if his life very depended on it.

Wind gave one last blow – and then he could blow no more. He was puffed out.

The storm clouds slowly cleared. Trees lifted their branches.

The gale gradually eased, and the children came out to play again.

Even the sharp little breezes stopped their gusty outbursts.

Everything slowly but surely became calm and still.

And then it was Sun's turn to try and remove the traveller's coat.

She sent her gentle sunbeams down to warm the battered Earth below.

Birds started singing again and bees started humming as they buzzed around flowers.

Mothers pegged the washing back on clothes lines.

The captains on the ships at sea told the passengers that they could go back to their swimming pools and deck chairs.

And still Sun kept shining brightly and warmly.

Meanwhile, Wind was watching the traveller very closely from behind the last cloud.

The traveller decided it was safe at last to leave his sheltered spot behind the roadside hedge.

He started walking along the road again on his way to the next town.

Warmer and warmer shone Sun.

The traveller had a bounce in his step because he was so happy that the Wind had blown itself out.

It wasn't long before the traveller started to feel warm.

He stopped and looked up at the brightening sky.

The clouds had blown away and in their place was a bright blue sky filled with sunshine.

Both Sun and Wind watched to see what he would do next.

Wind was about to see exactly what he didn't want to see.

'Oh no! The traveller is unbuttoning his coat and, now he is, oh no, he's taking it off!'

'And he's whistling happily as he walks along, carrying his coat on his arm! I've lost! I've lost!'

'Your quiet warm sunshine has had the power to win the contest, Sun.

I'm not happy, but you win!'

Wind growled and rumbled just a little with the breath he had left.

He knew he was well and truly beaten.

And off he went to blow somewhere else.

Sun kept warming the Earth below with her power, as she does every day.

Unless, of course, Wind decides to have another attempt at trying to remove the coats of travellers!

The Wind and the Sun is a famous fable by Aesop.

As the Wind and Sun proves to us, the moral of this story is that …

(Both readers together)

... being warm and friendly is far

better than being rough and pushy!

The Baby's Own Aesop (1908)
Illustration by Walter Crane

The Readers' Theatre series by *Ellie Hallett*

These **Readers' Theatre** stories have a major advantage in that everyone has equal reading time. Best of all, they are theatrical, immediately engaging and entertaining. Ellie Hallett's unique play-in-rows format, developed and trialled with great success in her own classrooms, combines expressive oral reading, active listening, peer teaching, vocabulary building, visualisation, and best of all, enjoyment.

ISBN	Title	Author	Price	E-book Price	QTY
9781921016455	Goldilocks and The Three Bears	Hallett, Ellie	9.95	9.95	
9781925398045	Jack and the Beanstalk	Hallett, Ellie	9.95	9.95	
9781925398069	The Fox and the Goat	Hallett, Ellie	9.95	9.95	
9781925398076	The Gingerbread Man	Hallett, Ellie	9.95	9.95	
9781925398052	Little Red Riding Hood and the Five Senses	Hallett, Ellie	9.95	9.95	
9781925398083	The Town Mouse and the Country Mouse	Hallett, Ellie	9.95	9.95	
9781925398014	The Two Travellers	Hallett, Ellie	9.95	9.95	
9781925398007	The Enormous Turnip	Hallett, Ellie	9.95	9.95	
9781925398090	The Hare and the Tortoise	Hallett, Ellie	9.95	9.95	
9781925398106	The Wind and the Sun	Hallett, Ellie	9.95	9.95	
9781925398113	The Three Wishes	Hallett, Ellie	9.95	9.95	
9781921016554	The Man, the Boy and the Donkey	Hallett, Ellie	9.95	9.95	
9781925398120	The Fox and the Crow	Hallett, Ellie	9.95	9.95	
9781920824921	Who Will Bell the Cat?	Hallett, Ellie	9.95	9.95	
9781925398021	The Ugly Duckling	Hallett, Ellie	9.95	9.95	

KNOWLEDGE
BOOKS AND SOFTWARE
PUBLISHING

www.kbs.com.au

Readers' Theatre